W9-BUX-540

Tiger Woods

by Elizabeth Sirimarco

Reading Consultant:
Dr. Robert Miller
Professor of Special Education
Minnesota State University

CAPSTONE BOOKS
an imprint of Capstone Press
Mankato, Minnesota

Capstone Books are published by Capstone Press
151 Good Counsel Drive, P.O. Box 669, Mankato, Minnesota 56002
http://www.capstone-press.com

Printed in the United States of America.

Library of Congress Cataloging-in-Publication Data
Sirimarco, Elizabeth, 1966–
Tiger Woods/by Elizabeth Sirimarco.
p. cm.—(Sports heroes)
Includes bibliographical references and index.
Summary: Examines the life and golfing accomplishments of Tiger Woods, the first golfer of African or Asian heritage to win a Major.
ISBN 0-7368-0581-8
1. Woods, Tiger—Juvenile literature. 2. Golfers—United States—Biography—juvenile literature. [1. Woods, Tiger. 2. Golfers. 3. Racially mixed people—Biography.] I. Title. II. Series.
GV964.W66 S57 2001
796.352'092—dc21
[B] 00-025636

Editorial Credits
Matt Doeden, editor; Timothy Halldin, cover designer and illustrator; Heidi Schoof and Kimberly Danger, photo researchers

Photo Credits
Allsport USA/David Cannon, 4, 6, 33; J.D. Cuban, 10, 26, 28, 30; Ken Levine, 12, 16; Andy Lyons, 14, 20; Rusty Jarrett, 23; Patrick Murphy-Racey, 24; Harry How, 37, 42; Craig Jones, 38
AP/World Wide Photos, cover; Bob Galbraith, 19; Scott Audette, 41
SportsChrome-USA/David Callow, 9; Frank Peters, 34

1 2 3 4 5 6 06 05 04 03 02 01

Table of Contents

Features

Chapter 1

Making History

It was Sunday, April 13, 1997. Tiger Woods was playing the last round of the Masters tournament in Augusta, Georgia. He had been a professional golfer for less than eight months. But he was already one of the sport's most popular stars. That day, he was trying to win the biggest Professional Golfers' Association (PGA) tournament of the year.

The Masters is one of the PGA's four "majors." These tournaments are the four most important events in professional golf. The other three majors are the PGA Championship, the British Open, and the U.S. Open. Tiger had dreamed of winning a major for most of his

Tiger entered the last round of the 1997 Masters with a nine-stroke lead.

On the front nine Thursday, I was just like anybody else. I played shaky, but I also played patient. From there, it evolved into one of my best ball-striking rounds, putting rounds, and management skills I've ever put together.
—Tiger Woods, AP, 4/14/97

life. His dream was about to come true. Thousands of fans had gathered at the Augusta National Golf Club to watch him. Millions more watched on TV.

The Masters lasts for four days. Golfers play one round each day. They begin on Thursday. Tiger began the first round poorly. He shot a score of 40 on the first nine holes. That score was four over par. Tiger knew that he had to play better in order to win. Tiger shot six under par on the next nine holes. His score for the day was 70. He was in fourth place.

Tiger's scores improved as the tournament continued. Friday, he had a score of 66. Saturday, he shot a 65. Those scores were among the best in the tournament's history. Tiger was in control. He was nine strokes ahead of the second-place golfer. Only one day remained in the tournament.

Tiger did not disappoint his fans on Sunday. The record tournament score at the Masters was 271. Tiger could tie the record with a score of 70 for Sunday's round. Instead, Tiger

Tiger won the 1997 Masters with a record score of 270.

shot a 69 to break the record. His final score was 270. At age 21, he was the youngest Masters champion in history. Tiger's dream had come true.

About Tiger Woods

Tiger is one of the most popular golfers in the world. His success has increased young people's interest in the game. His success also has encouraged an interest in golf by people of many ethnic backgrounds. Tiger is African American and Asian. Before Tiger, most golf stars were older than 25. Few golfers were from minority ethnic backgrounds. Tiger showed young people of many ethnic backgrounds that they could be excellent golfers.

Tiger also is successful off the golf course. He is one of the world's most popular and recognized athletes. He endorses many products such as Nike sportswear and Buick cars. Tiger even has a video game named for him. These endorsements earn Tiger millions of dollars each year.

Career Statistics

Tiger Woods

PGA Finishes

Year	1st	2nd	3rd	Top 10
1996	2	0	2	5
1997	4	1	1	9
1998	1	2	2	13
1999	8	1	2	16
Total	15	4	7	43

CHAPTER 2

The Early Years

Tiger was born December 30, 1975, in Cypress, California. His parents' names are Earl and Kultida. Tiger's parents named him Eldrick at birth. Earl had fought in the Vietnam War (1954–1975). During the war, Earl met a South Vietnamese soldier named Nguyen Phong. Earl nicknamed Phong "Tiger" because he was so brave. Phong saved Earl's life twice. Earl called his son Tiger in honor of his friend.

Tiger's parents met in Thailand during the war. Kultida was from Thailand. Earl brought Kultida back to the United States after his war service was over. They married in 1969.

Earl Woods gave Tiger his nickname.

Learning Golf

Earl began playing golf shortly before Tiger was born. He wanted to practice to become better. Earl set up a large net in his garage so he could practice hitting balls.

When Tiger was a baby, Earl sometimes took him into the garage while he practiced. Tiger would watch Earl hit golf balls. One day, Tiger picked up one of his father's clubs. He put a ball in place and swung the club. Tiger hit the ball perfectly. He was less than 1 year old at the time.

From that moment, Tiger loved to play golf. Earl bought him a set of children's clubs. But the clubs still were too big for Tiger. Earl used a saw to shorten the clubs. Tiger learned to play golf with these clubs. By age 2, he played and won his first children's golf tournament. He soon appeared on TV shows such as "The CBS Evening News" and "The Mike Douglas Show." Tiger displayed his golfing abilities on these shows.

Tiger became a great golfer at a young age.

Tiger and Jack Nicklaus are among the most popular PGA players of all time.

Grade School

In 1981, Tiger started kindergarten. His teacher believed that he was very smart for his age. She thought Tiger was smart enough to skip ahead one grade. But Tiger did not want to move to first grade. He did not want to leave his friends.

At age 6, Tiger entered his first international tournament. He played in the Junior World

Championship in the 10-and-under division. Tiger finished the tournament in eighth place. All of the boys who finished ahead of him were 10 years old. Tiger also recorded his first hole in one that year.

Tiger returned to the Junior World Championship in the following years. He won the championship twice. At age 10, Tiger moved up a division. He played against 11- and 12-year-olds. He won again.

In 1986, 11-year-old Tiger often read *Golf Digest* magazine. That year, the magazine published a list of Jack Nicklaus's achievements. Many people believed Nicklaus was the greatest golfer ever. The list showed how old Nicklaus was when he achieved each of his accomplishments. Tiger cut out the magazine article and saved it. He wanted to do everything Nicklaus had done. He also wanted to achieve these accomplishments at a younger age.

Tiger remained a good student throughout school. Kultida never let him practice golf until he finished his homework. Tiger's grades were always among the best in his class.

PING

Chapter 3

Playing to Win

Tiger's golf skills improved as he grew older. Many golf experts believed he could become a professional golfer.

Tiger tried not to let the attention change him. He still wanted to be like other kids his age. He liked to eat junk food, watch TV, and spend time with his friends. But Tiger knew that he was different. At age 15, he said that he wanted to become the Michael Jordan of golf. He wanted to be as good at golf as Jordan was at basketball.

Golf experts noticed Tiger when he was still in his early teens.

My goal is to obviously be the best. I know that's a very lofty goal ... I expect nothing but the best for myself.
—Tiger Woods, AP, 4/16/97

High School Years

Tiger competed in junior tournaments throughout high school. These tournaments include players younger than 18 years old. He also played for Western High School's golf team. At age 15, Tiger won the U.S. Junior Amateur event. *Golf Digest* ranked him the number one junior player in the country.

In 1992, Tiger played in his first professional event. He was 16 years old. He played as an amateur in the Los Angeles Open. Amateur golfers do not earn money for playing in tournaments. Tiger gained valuable experience by competing with professionals. Later that year, Tiger won the U.S. Junior Amateur again. No golfer had ever won this event twice.

Tiger's success continued on the golf course and in the classroom. At 17, Tiger won a third straight U.S. Junior Amateur title. He graduated from high school in 1994 with an A average. His golfing achievements and good grades

During high school, Tiger played in both high school tournaments and in junior tournaments.

TIGERS

A Hero's Hero

Lee Elder

Tiger Woods looked up to several famous golfers as he grew up. But a less famous golfer also was one of his personal heroes.

Lee Elder was one of the first African Americans to succeed in professional golf. He began his professional career in the late 1950s. Elder faced a great deal of prejudice early in his career. Many people at that time did not believe African Americans should play golf. In 1975, Elder became the first African American golfer to play in the Masters. Today, he competes in PGA Senior Tour events.

earned him the Dial Award. This award honored him for being the top high school student-athlete in the United States.

Colleges around the country wanted Tiger to play golf for their golf teams. Stanford University in California was among these colleges. Tiger thought that Stanford was a good place to get an education. He accepted a golf scholarship from Stanford. The scholarship allowed Tiger to attend college for free by playing on Stanford's golf team.

Growing Fame

In 1994, Tiger played in the U.S. Amateur tournament. He was 18 years old. Most of the other players were much older. They had years of experience. They were the best amateur golfers in the world.

Tiger trailed in the tournament by as many as six strokes. No one had ever come back to win the tournament after trailing by that many strokes. But Tiger believed in himself. He came back to tie the leader on the 16th hole of the last round of play. On the 17th hole, Tiger decided to gamble. The 17th hole had a small pond in front of the green. Most players hit short drives in front of the water. But Tiger decided to try going over the water. He would have a chance at a birdie if he made the shot. But he would lose his chance to win the tournament if he missed.

Tiger's gamble worked. The ball landed past the water and rolled back. It stopped only 3 feet (1 meter) from the pond's edge. Tiger then made a 19-foot (5.8-meter) putt for a birdie. Tiger became the U.S. Amateur champion. He was the youngest golfer ever to win the tournament. He also was the first African American golfer to win.

Tiger's hometown of Cypress held a dinner to honor his victory. President Bill Clinton wrote him a letter to congratulate him. Newspapers such as *The New York Times* and *USA Today* featured Tiger on their front pages. Tiger was becoming a star.

Tiger needed a great comeback to win the 1994 Junior Amateur tournament.

Entering College

Tiger entered Stanford in 1994. His Stanford teammates knew that he was a great golfer. But they treated him the same as they treated the other team members. Older players made him and the other first-year students on the team carry their luggage. They also teased him. They called him "Urkel" after a character from the TV show *Family Matters*.

Tiger had a good first year. He studied hard. He also played well for Stanford. Tiger earned the Player of the Year award as the PAC-10 conference's best golfer. He also was named to the NCAA's All-American team.

That summer, Tiger played in the Masters for the first time. He was the first African American to play in the event since Lee Elder in 1975. Tiger did not win the Masters. But the professional golfers began to notice his talent.

Tiger won two PAC-10 Player of the Year awards while at Stanford.

The Greatest Amateur

Tiger won the U.S. Amateur tournament again in 1995. Many people believed he was ready to become a professional golfer. But he wanted to continue to play as an amateur. Tiger had one more goal. He wanted to become the greatest amateur golfer of all time. Tiger still kept his list of Jack Nicklaus's achievements. Nicklaus had never won three straight U.S. Amateur tournaments. Tiger wanted to try.

Tiger played another year for Stanford. Again, he won the Pac-10 Player of the Year award. He was again named to the All-American team. He also led Stanford to the NCAA men's golf championship.

Tiger's final amateur event was the 1996 U.S. Amateur. He struggled early in the tournament. He trailed the leaders by as many as five strokes. But Tiger came back and won the title on a playoff hole. He had achieved his goal. He was ready to become a professional golfer.

Tiger won the 1996 U.S. Amateur on a playoff hole. It was his last amateur event.

Chapter 4

Going Pro

Tiger announced that he was turning professional only days after winning the U.S. Amateur. He made the announcement at a press conference in Milwaukee, Wisconsin. Later that week, he played in his first tournament as a professional at the Milwaukee Open.

Tiger's decision meant he could no longer play golf for Stanford. Professionals are not allowed to play on college teams. His decision also meant he had to leave school. He did not have time for his studies on the pro tour. Tiger promised his parents that he would go back to college someday.

Tiger announced that he was turning pro before the 1996 Milwaukee Open.

Tiger's first professional victory was at the 1996 Las Vegas Invitational.

Pro Beginnings

Tiger did not play well at the Milwaukee Open. A large crowd followed him around throughout the tournament. Everyone wanted to see him play. But Tiger finished the tournament in 60th place. Some people were disappointed. But Tiger was happy to have finished his first tournament as a professional.

Tiger's play improved as he played in more tournaments. He finished 11th, fifth, and third in his next three tournaments.

Tiger earned his first tournament win at the Las Vegas Invitational. It was his fifth pro tournament. Several weeks later, he won the Disney World/Oldsmobile Classic. Tiger had finished among the top 10 in five of his first seven tournaments. He won two of them.

The world of golf had noticed Tiger. He was named PGA Rookie of the Year as golf's best first-year professional. *Sports Illustrated* magazine named Tiger the 1996 Sportsman of the Year. Record crowds came to the tournaments he played.

Businesses also noticed Tiger's popularity. Many asked Tiger to endorse their products. Soon, Tiger appeared in advertisements for companies including Nike sportswear and Titleist golf balls. He earned millions of dollars for endorsing these products. He became one of the richest athletes in history.

The only thing I can say about my game is I go out and give it everything I've got. Sometimes, I'll shoot like I did last year. Sometimes, it'll be like this year.
—Tiger Woods, AP, 4/13/98

Rise and Fall

For Tiger, 1997 was an even better year. He began the year by winning the Mercedes Championship. In April, he won the Masters. Tiger also won three other tournaments. Other professional golfers voted him the 1997 PGA Player of the Year.

Tiger's popularity was increasing throughout the world. But some people did not like Tiger. Some professional golfers thought he did not work as hard as he could. Tiger would not talk to reporters when he had bad days. Tiger even turned down an invitation to visit President Clinton at the White House. He went on a vacation instead.

Tiger struggled in 1998. He won only one event that year. Some people believed Tiger was having trouble handling the money and fame golf had brought him. But Tiger said he just wanted to improve as a golfer. He knew his golf game was not perfect.

Large crowds followed Tiger throughout the 1997 season.

Chapter 5

Tiger Woods Today

Tiger came back from his difficult 1998 season. In 1999, he won eight events. This was the most events one player had won in a year since 1974. One of the events was the PGA Championship. Tiger's success in 1999 earned him another PGA Player of the Year award.

Tiger also played on the United States' 1999 Ryder Cup team. He and his teammates played against Europe's best golfers in this match. The U.S. team came from behind to win on the last day of the event. Tiger won

Tiger won eight events in 1999.

his last match to help the United States earn the victory.

Six Straight

In February 2000, Tiger was in the middle of one of the greatest streaks in golf history. Starting in 1999, he had won five straight events. Tiger's next event was the Pebble Beach Pro-Am in Pebble Beach, California. A win would make him the first golfer to win six straight events since Ben Hogan in 1948.

Tiger's chances did not look good going into the tournament's final round. He trailed the leaders by five strokes. Tiger's luck got worse as the day went on. He trailed tournament leader Matt Gogel by seven strokes with only seven holes to play. But Gogel had trouble on several of the holes that day. Gogel's struggles gave Tiger a chance to come back. Tiger felt he could give himself a chance to win. He just needed to play well enough on the final holes.

Tiger won six straight events from late 1999 through early 2000.

It's just interesting that here people talk about the streak, rather than the shots I'm hitting or the putts I make here and there. And I think that's more important than the streak, because that's what keeps it alive.
—Tiger Woods, AP, 2/10/2000

On the 15th hole, Tiger hit a long drive on a par-5 hole. The drive set up an eagle putt. Tiger made the putt. This helped him to a score of eight under par for the day.

Tiger finished his round with a birdie on the 18th hole. Tiger then had to watch Gogel play the last hole. On the 18th green, Gogel had a chance to force a playoff hole. He had to make a 10-foot (3-meter) putt. But Gogel missed the putt and Tiger won his sixth straight event.

Off the Golf Course

Tiger remains close with his parents. Earl and Kultida often travel to tournaments to watch Tiger play. Earl even wrote a book about raising Tiger. The book's title is *Training a Tiger.*

Tiger is committed to helping children when he is not golfing. He started the Tiger Woods Foundation for this purpose. The foundation has given millions of dollars to

Tiger's parents often travel to tournaments around the country to watch him play.

organizations that help children. Through the foundation, Tiger teaches golf clinics for children in inner cities around the United States. Tiger gives private lessons to 25 children from the community during each clinic. Other golf instructors teach another 100 children. Tiger believes the clinics give the children a chance to succeed at golf.

Tiger also gives speeches to groups of children around the United States. He tells them about his life. He talks about his success in golf and how he worked to achieve his goals. He answers the children's questions. Tiger also tries to teach children how to set goals and succeed.

Tiger teaches children how to golf at clinics around the United States.

Career Highlights

1975—Tiger Woods is born on December 30 in Cypress, California.

1981—Tiger records his first hole in one.

1983—Tiger wins the Junior World Championship.

1987—Tiger is undefeated in southern California golf tournaments. He wins 30 tournaments.

1991—At age 15, Tiger becomes the youngest golfer to win the Junior Amateur.

1992—Tiger takes part in his first PGA tournament.

1993—Tiger wins the Junior Amateur for the third year in a row.

1994—Tiger becomes the youngest golfer to win the U.S. Amateur. He also enters Stanford University.

1995—Tiger wins his second U.S. Amateur title.

1996—Tiger leads Stanford to an NCAA championship. He earns his first professional victory at the Las Vegas Invitational.

1997—Tiger wins the Masters tournament. He is named PGA Player of the Year.

1999—Tiger wins eight PGA events. He wins his second PGA Player of the Year award.

2000—Tiger becomes the first golfer to win six events in a row since Ben Hogan in 1948.

Words to Know

amateur (AM-uh-chur)—someone who participates in a sport without being paid

endorse (en-DORSS)—to sponsor a product by appearing in advertisements

minority (mye-NOR-uh-tee)—a group of people of a particular race group living among a larger group of a different race

prejudice (PREJ-uh-diss)—an unfair opinion based on a person's race, religion, or other characteristic

professional (pruh-FESH-uh-nuhl)—someone who is paid to participate in a sport

scholarship (SKOL-ur-ship)—a grant that helps a student pay for college

To Learn More

Dougherty, Terri. *Tiger Woods.* Jam Session. Edina, Minn.: Abdo, 1999.

Durbin, William C. *Tiger Woods.* Black Americans of Achievement. Philadelphia: Chelsea House Publishers, 1998.

Lace, William W. *Tiger Woods: Star Golfer.* Sports Reports. Springfield, N.J.: Enslow Publishers, 1999.

Rambeck, Richard. *Tiger Woods.* Chanhassen, Minn.: Child's World, 1999.

Useful Addresses

Canadian Junior Golf Association
33 Gaby Court
Richmond Hill, ON L4C 8X1
Canada

PGA Junior Tournaments
Tournament Department
P.O. Box 109601
Palm Beach Gardens, FL 33410

Tiger Woods (fan mail)
c/o IMG
1 Erie View Plaza
Cleveland, OH 44114

Internet Sites

PGA of America
http://www.pga.com

Tiger Tales
http://www.texnews.com/tiger

Tiger Woods Bio, Stats, and Results
http://www.pgatour.com/players/intro/8793.html

Tiger Woods Official Website
http://www.tigerwoods.com

Index